# Earth's Weather

by Christine Wolf

PEARSON
Scott
Foresman

# What is weather?

Weather happens because of changes in Earth's temperature. Days can be hot or cold, wet or dry. Different kinds of clouds and wind are also a part of weather.

# What makes weather wet or dry?

Rain, hail, and snow are kinds of wet weather. Clouds are made of lots of water droplets and tiny bits of ice. The clouds get big and heavy.

The droplets can fall to the ground as rain when the air is warm. They may fall to the ground as sleet or snow when the air is cold.

Some places do not get a lot of rain. These places have very dry weather. It is called a drought when a place receives less rain than normal. Plants and animals may not have enough water during a drought.

Some places are wet and green in winter.
In the summer they can be dry and brown.

# The Water Cycle

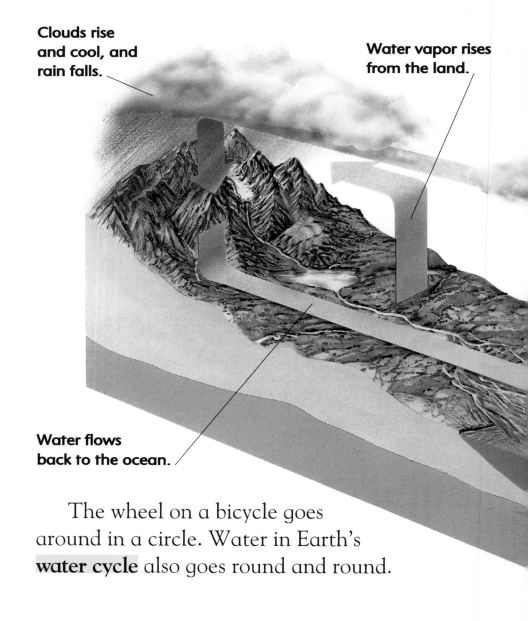

**Clouds rise and cool, and rain falls.**

**Water vapor rises from the land.**

**Water flows back to the ocean.**

The wheel on a bicycle goes around in a circle. Water in Earth's **water cycle** also goes round and round.

Earth's water keeps moving between the oceans, the sky, and the land. Water **evaporates** from the ocean and rises to form clouds.

The water vapor in clouds gets cold and changes, or **condenses,** back to water droplets. The water droplets fall back to the ground.

Rain gathers in rivers and runs to oceans. The Sun heats the oceans and the cycle begins again.

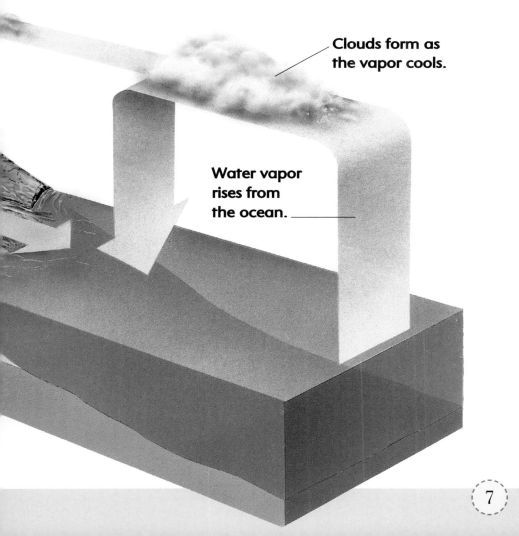

Clouds form as the vapor cools.

Water vapor rises from the ocean.

# The Four Seasons

Many parts of the world have four seasons. They are spring, summer, fall, and winter. Each season has its own weather.

spring

fall

summer

winter

The four seasons together last one year. In each season days can be longer or shorter. Animals and plants behave differently in each season too.

# Spring

Spring is the season of change and growth. Often, spring has rainy days and cool nights. Small plants begin to grow in spring.

You may see new green leaves on trees. Many baby animals are born in the spring. Lots of flowers bloom. What is spring like where you live?

# Summer

Summer is often hot and sunny. Summer has more hours of daylight than spring. The Sun is high in the sky. Many people like to be outside in the summer.

Baby animals grow up in the summer. Many fruits and vegetables ripen in the summer. What is summer like where you live?

# Fall

In fall the temperature cools down. There are fewer hours of daylight than in summer. Leaves may change color, and some leaves fall off the trees.

In the fall many animals begin to prepare for the winter. Some animals, such as squirrels, gather and store food.

Other animals, such as Canada geese, travel, or **migrate,** to different places. What is fall like where you live?

# Winter

Winter is the coldest season. In many places, snow falls, lakes and ponds freeze, and icicles form. Winter has the fewest hours of daylight. The Sun is low in the sky.

Some animals
hibernate in winter.
**Hibernate** means to
hide away and sleep.
Animals that hibernate
fatten up so their bodies
can stay warm as they
sleep. What is winter
like where you live?

# Dangerous Weather

Sometimes wet weather can be dangerous. Thunderstorms often form on hot summer days.

They can bring heavy rain, hail, thunder, and lightning.

Lightning is a flash of light in the sky. Thunder is the sound that follows lightning.

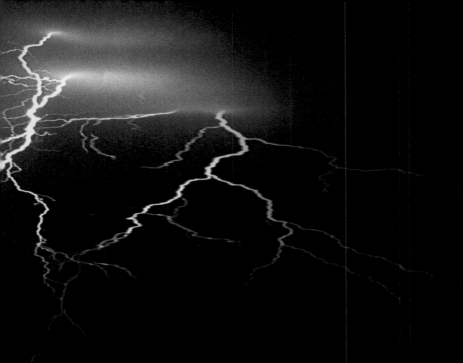

# Staying Safe In A Thunderstorm

Staying safe from lightning means finding shelter in a building. It also helps to stay away from water, metal objects, and trees.

# Staying Safe In a Tornado

**Tornadoes** are made up of strong winds that move in a circle. Air inside a tornado acts like a giant straw. Everything in a tornado's path gets sucked up into the sky.

Tornadoes can be unexpected. If you are ever caught in a tornado you should find shelter indoors. You should stay in the basement or under the stairs. Keep away from windows, water, and metal objects.

# Staying Safe In a Hurricane

When many thunderstorms join together, a **hurricane** may form. Heavy rains fall during hurricanes. Strong winds blow and knock down buildings and trees.

People who live near the beach move away from the water when a hurricane is coming. They stay away from the huge waves. People board up windows and bring inside things that might fly around.

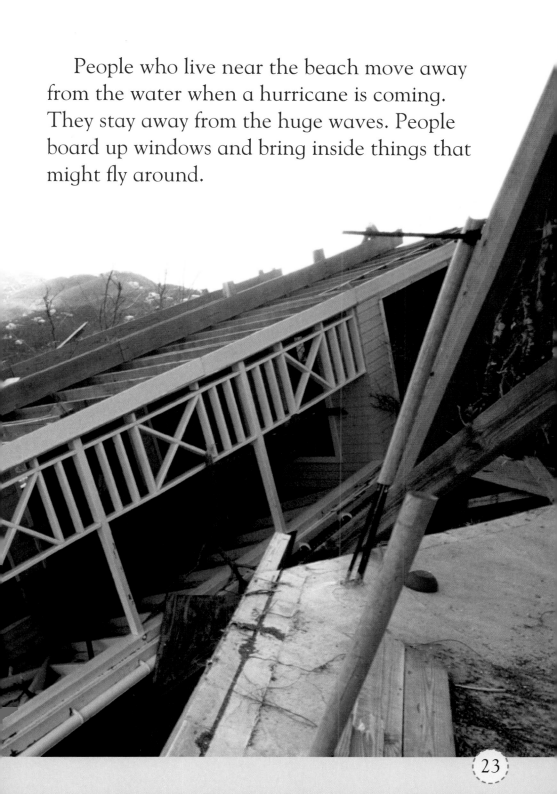

# Glossary

**condense**    to change from water vapor to water droplets

**evaporate**    to change from water to water vapor

**hibernate**    to hide away and sleep through winter

**hurricane**    a very strong storm that starts over the ocean

**lightning**    a flash of light in the sky

**migrate**    to move to a warmer place when winter is coming

**tornado**    a circling column of air

**water cycle**    the movement of water from Earth to the sky and back again